ARKANA

A Gift of Healing

Frances Vaughan, Ph.D., is a psychologist in the clini-
cal faculty of the University of California. She is the
author of *Awakening Intuition* and *The Inward Arc: Healing and Wholeness in Psychotherapy and Spirituality* and
co-editor, with Roger Walsh, of *Beyond Ego: Trans-
personal Dimensions in Psychology*.

Roger Walsh, M.D., Ph.D., is a professor of psychiatry
and philosophy at the University of California. He is
co-editor of *Beyond Health and Normality: Explorations of
Exceptional Psychological Well-Being* and of *Meditation:
Ancient and Contemporary Perspectives*. He is also author
of *Staying Alive: The Psychology of Human Survival*,
which discusses the psychological causes, costs and
potential cures of current global crises. His work has
received twenty national and international awards.

Jane English's photographs have been published in
translations of two of the Chinese Taoist classics, *Tao
Te Ching* by Lao Tsu and *Inner Chapters*, by Chuang
Tsu.

A Gift of Healing is the third in a series of books drawn
from *A Course in Miracles*, edited by Frances Vaughan
and Roger Walsh. The first two volumes are *Accept
This*

A GIFT OF HEALING

SELECTIONS FROM
A Course in Miracles

EDITED BY

Frances Vaughan, Ph.D.
and
Roger Walsh, M.D., Ph.D.

PHOTOGRAPHS BY
Jane English, Ph.D.

ARKANA
PENGUIN BOOKS

This book is dedicated to
the healing of hearts and minds

ARKANA

Published by the Penguin Group
Penguin Books Ltd, 27 Wrights Lane, London W8 5TZ, England
Penguin Books USA Inc., 375 Hudson Street, New York, New York 10014, USA
Penguin Books Australia Ltd, Ringwood, Victoria, Australia
Penguin Books Canada Ltd, 10 Alcorn Avenue, Toronto, Ontario, Canada M4V 3B
Penguin Books (NZ) Ltd, 182–190 Wairau Road, Auckland 10, New Zealand

Penguin Books Ltd, Registered Offices: Harmondsworth, Middlesex, England

First published in USA by Jeremy P. Tarcher, Inc. 1988
Published in Arkana 1990
3 5 7 9 10 8 6 4 2

Printed in England by Clays Ltd, St Ives plc

CONTENTS

INTRODUCTION

No one would deny humankind's great need for healing. All around us in this war-torn world the evidence is clear for anyone willing to see it. On a grand scale one sees wars, famine, disaster, and disease; on a small scale the countless little hurts, psychological and physical, spiritual and emotional, that we know so well. Sickness and death, pain and sorrow, separation and loss are clearly part of our human condition. Of course, there are also periods of great love, joy, and peace, and some of us are fortunate enough to experience many of these. But even into the most fortunate lives pain intrudes at times.

Dissatisfaction with our lives, the limits of the body, and the inescapability of death have been central themes of the great religions. In the immensity of the universe we seem "as dust," say the ancient biblical psalms. Our lives are "but toil and trouble; they are soon gone. . . . they come to an end like a sigh" (Psalm 90). "What man can live and not see death?" (Psalm 89). In the Bhagavad Gita (the "Hindu Bible"), the wise are said to be those capable of "seeing the defects in birth, death, old age, sickness, and suffering." "Unenlightened existence is inherently unsatisfactory," states the Buddha's First Noble Truth. Recently, this sentiment has been echoed by contemporary existentialists who see anxiety, angst, and despair as inescapable elements of human life.

But the great religions do not stop with merely recognizing the pain of our usual existence. They go further, to declare that we can escape the pain, and they offer us means for this escape. In fact, every great religion claims that our suffering is the product of ignorance and illusion. Suffering, they say, results when we forget who we really are—Children of God, Atman, Buddha Nature or one with the Tao—and mistake ourselves for limited beings, skin-encapsulated egos trapped inside fragile, transitory bodies. We suffer ultimately, say the great religions, from a case of mistaken identity, a false self-concept, an erroneous image that is but a pale shadow of our true limitless being. We live not in reality, but in illusion—maya or samsara. We have forgotten who we really are and misperceive our nightmares of sickness and suffering for reality, while our true nature abides unchanged and unchangeable as pure radiant sat-chit-ananda: limitless consciousness, being, and bliss.

From this viewpoint, the sickness and suffering that seem inescapable from our egocentric perspective are recognized as illusions, incapable of harming our true Self in any way. All suffering is seen as but a dream. It follows that the healing of sickness and pain involves awakening from our collective dream and remembering who we really are. This awakening is known in various traditions as salvation, satori, liberation, or enlightenment. It need not involve changes in our physical circumstances because our pain and sickness, and even the bodies in which they occur, are parts of a dream. We need not seek to change our true nature, which is actually unchangeable. Rather we need only recognize, remember, and awaken to it, and the nightmare of suffering ceases to exert its apparent effects on us. As *A Course in Miracles* says: "Those who seek the light are merely covering their eyes. The light is in them now. Enlightenment is but a recognition, not a change at all." This recognition has been the goal of spiritual teachers and traditions across countless cultures and centuries, and each has offered a path and practice by which it can occur.

A Course in Miracles represents one form of this timeless wisdom, a path to enlightenment, a guide to awakening, a gift of healing. As such it can be seen as a contemporary version of the "perennial wisdom," that common core of wisdom at the heart of the great religions.

Like other forms of the perennial wisdom, the *Course* recognizes the universality of pain in human existence and the universal need for healing. It therefore offers us a path of healing and awakening by which our dreams of suffering can be recognized for what they are, and our true nature can be remembered.

In offering this path, the *Course* makes a diagnosis of our condition, identifies its causes, and presents a treatment plan. It emphasizes that our dreams are perpetuated by unhealthy habits, desires, and states of mind such as fear, anger, and attack. When we let these go, says the *Course,* we awaken from the dream and recognize ourselves as we have always been: children of God, limitless, blissful, loving, and free from suffering of any kind.

The means for this healing involves a systematic practice of mental habits that reduce and ultimately eliminate painful mind states. The *Course* encourages us to exchange anger for forgiveness, fear for love, and curse for blessing. In short, it advises us to substitute peaceful, loving states for angry, painful ones. This is no small task; countless people have devoted their lives to this aim and have found it to be a forbidding challenge. But *A Course in Miracles* claims to offer a gentle path in which this task of healing and awakening is made as easy as possible, demanding no sacrifice of any kind. For how could it be a sacrifice, asks the *Course,* to substitute the peace and joy of reality for the painful illusions of the ego?

The *Course's* view of healing, then, is radically different from the usual views of the world. The world sees sickness and healing as originating in the body; the *Course* sees them as originating in the mind. "Sickness is of the mind," it repeats again and again. It is the mind which is really in need of healing.

From the perspective of the perennial wisdom this

radically different claim makes perfect sense. For if our true nature or self remains unchanged and joyous while part of the mind dreams of being trapped in a finite, suffering body, then an awakening of the mind is needed, rather than a change in the body. The body is merely a fragment of a dream, which we have mistaken for our Self. The *Course* therefore offers a path of healing for our minds that will allow us to awaken from this dream of sickness, suffering, and separation from God.

The *Course* was written through a process of inner dictation by a very reluctant academic psychologist, Helen Schuchman. Although she had an intense childhood yearning for religious understanding, she had long ago despaired of finding it and described herself as a Jewish atheist.

She was assisted during the writing by her colleague, William Thetford. Both were successful professors of medical psychology at Columbia University in New York. Neither had any intention of writing anything religious. Indeed, their lives and work were hardly models of spiritual well-being. They were caught up in the harried and often vicious competition and infighting that can occur in prestigious academic centers. Their relationships were certainly in need of healing, and they lived with significant personal and interpersonal strife. Yet as the *Course* says, "Tolerance for pain may be high, but it is not without limit. Eventually everyone realizes, however dimly, that there must be a better way."

That realization came to Bill Thetford one day when he suddenly announced to Helen, "There must be a better way of living, and I'm determined to find it." Helen responded, "I agree, and I'll help you find it."

A few weeks later, Helen started having a series of intense visual images. So vivid were these images that initially Helen feared she might be losing her sanity. However, with Bill's encouragement, she allowed them to unfold and they proved to be personally meaningful as well as helpful to others.

Finally, at the end of three months, Helen heard an

inner voice saying, "This is a course in miracles. Please take notes." Terrified once again that she was losing her mind, Helen resisted at first, but Bill finally convinced her to take down in shorthand the words she was hearing. Thus began a six-year collaborative process of transcribing and typing Helen's dictation—and *A Course in Miracles* was born. With its emphasis on healing, and particularly on healing relationships, the *Course* was clearly the guide to a better way of living that Helen and Bill had agreed to seek together. A fuller account of this process of birthing the *Course* is available in the book *Journey Without Distance.*

The *Course* itself consists of three books. The first is a text that lays out the thought system; the second is a practical workbook with a lesson for each day of the year; and the third is a teacher's manual that clarifies terms and discusses some of the principles of teaching. Two smaller booklets on psychotherapy and prayer, similarly scribed, are also available.

The language of the *Course* is traditionally Christian, reminiscent of the King James Bible. Some words and phrases sound dated, and the masculine pronoun is used exclusively. People who find the language initially offputting may want to personally translate terms that are difficult for them by substituting others, for example, "liberation" for "salvation," or "Child of God" for "Son of God."

However, when the initial antipathy to the traditional language passes, the poetic beauty of the language and the profound impact of the message are unveiled and free to work their transformations on the reader. Indeed, the quality of writing has been compared to some of the great works of English literature, and much of the *Course* is written in iambic pentameter like Shakespearean blank verse.

In Christian language and metaphor, the *Course* transmits the perennial wisdom in a way that makes it available to many people who would not otherwise be able to hear it. Yet the *Course* also acknowledges the value and validity of other paths and makes no claims for exclusivity. Indeed, its message of healing for all people argues against excluding anyone.

Because its message is universal, the *Course* echoes themes and ideas found at the core of the great religions. It also contains philosophical and psychological insights on a par with both ancient wisdom and recent research. In short, the *Course* is an extremely rich, yet eminently practical path to healing and awakening. However, profound ideas follow one another in such rapid and poetic succession that it can be difficult to absorb more than a little at a time. Therefore, it is sometimes valuable to select brief excerpts for closer, more leisurely study, permitting the reader to more fully appreciate their impact and to focus on particular themes. This is the aim of *A Gift of Healing*.

The quotations included here focus specifically on healing. From the vast richness of the *Course*, we have selected those lines that seem to us most profound, moving, and poetic. But just as a few notes of melody cannot convey the majesty of a symphony, no selection can convey the breadth, depth, or many dimensions of *A Course in Miracles*. For that, one must turn to the original, and our hope is that *A Gift of Healing* will inspire those not already familiar with the *Course* to explore it directly.

A Course in Miracles has had an important influence on our lives, and we are grateful for the opportunity to share it in this way. We hope that the following passages will convey some of the beauty and benefits of the *Course*, and that they will offer to all who read them a gift of healing.

1

THE DESIRE FOR HEALING

The health of our bodies and the state of our world reflect our desires and defenses, fantasies and fears. If we would be healed we must relinquish these unhealthly motives and replace them with the desire for healing. We must also relinquish mental habits—such as anger, attack, and the sense of individual specialness—that separate us from others. Indeed, this sense of separation *is* our sickness.

The *Course* emphasizes that healing cannot be for ourselves alone, for in reality we are not alone and separate. We must help each other, and thus relationships become a central focus for healing. The *Course* says, "In your brother you but see yourself." Our desire to find a better way therefore becomes a driving force for healing both ourselves and others.

As we ourselves are healed, we provide an example for others. And as we desire to help and heal others, we ourselves are also healed. The result is that relationships become "a temple of healing" in which healing is recognized as a collaborative venture that leads to the recognition of our underlying unity.

Your function in this world is healing.

The Decision to Heal

The decision to heal and to be healed
is the first step toward recognizing
what you truly want.
Every attack is a step away from this,
and every healing thought
brings it closer.

To be healed is to pursue one goal,
because you have accepted only one
and want but one.

Nothing is harmful or beneficent
apart from what you wish.
It is your wish
that makes it what it is
in its effects on you.

There is no miracle
you cannot have
when you desire healing.
But there is no miracle
that can be given you
unless you want it.

Your function on earth is healing. . . .
As long as you believe you have other functions,
so long will you need correction.
For this belief is the destruction of peace.

Healing will always stand aside
when it would be seen as threat.
The instant it is welcome it is there.
Where healing has been given
it will be received.

You have been called,
together with your brother,
to the most holy function
this world contains.
It is the only one
that has no limits,
and reaches out
to every broken fragment of the Sonship
with healing and uniting comfort.
This is offered you,
in your holy relationship.
Accept it here,
and you will give
as you have accepted.

Suffice it, then, that you have work to do
to play your part.
The ending must remain obscure to you
until your part is done.
It does not matter.
For your part is still
what all the rest depends on.

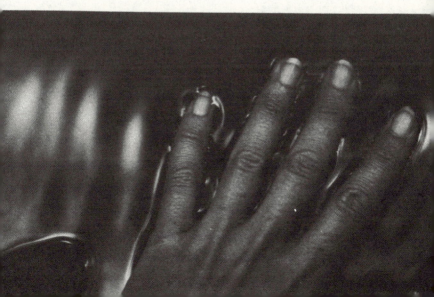

The Conditions of Healing

Healing is the effect of minds that join,
as sickness comes from minds that separate.

If you are unwilling
to perceive an appeal for help
as what it is,
it is because you are unwilling
to give help and receive it.
To fail to recognize a call for help
is to refuse to help.
Would you maintain that you do not need it?
Yet this is what you are maintaining
when you refuse to recognize a brother's appeal,
for only by answering his appeal
can you be helped.

Your interpretations of your brother's needs
are your interpretations of yours.
By giving help you are asking for it.

It may help someone to point out
where he is heading,
but the point is lost
unless he is also helped
to change his direction.
The unhealed healer cannot do this for him,
since he cannot do it for himself.
The only meaningful contribution
the healer can make
is to present an example
of one whose direction
has been changed for him,
and who no longer believes
in nightmares of any kind.

Healing perceives nothing in the healer
that everyone else does not share with him.

Healing sees no specialness at all.
It does not come from pity
but from love.

There is no sadness
where a miracle has come to heal.
And nothing more than just one instant
of your love without attack is necessary
that all this occur.
In that one instant you are healed,
and in that single instant
is all healing done.

Healing reflects our joint will.
This is obvious when you consider
what healing is for.
Healing is the way in which
the separation is overcome.

You have learned your need of healing.
Would you bring anything else to the Sonship,
recognizing your need of healing for yourself?

Accept the miracle of healing,
and it will go forth
because of what it is.
It is its nature to extend itself
the instant it is born.
And it is born
the instant it is offered and received.

No one can ask another to be healed.
But he can let himself be healed,
and thus offer the other
what he has received.
Who can bestow upon another
what he does not have?
And who can share
what he denies himself?

If you wish only to be healed,
you heal.
Your single purpose makes this possible.
But if you are afraid of healing,
then it cannot come through you.
The only thing that is required for a healing
is lack of fear.
The fearful are not healed,
and cannot heal.
This does not mean the conflict
must be gone forever from your mind to heal.
For if it were,
there were no need for healing then.
But it does mean, if only for an instant,
you love without attack.
An instant is sufficient.
Miracles wait not on time.

The only way to heal
is to be healed.

Those who are healed
become the instruments
of healing.

Healing One Another

Healing is a collaborative venture.

It is impossible that anyone be healed alone.
In sickness must he be apart and separate.
But healing is his own decision to be one again,
and to accept his Self.

Fail not your brothers, or you fail yourself.
Look lovingly on them, that they may know
that they are part of you, and you of them.

From you can come their rest.
From you can rise a world
they will rejoice to look upon,
and where their hearts are glad.
In you there is a vision
that extends to all of them,
and covers them in gentleness and light.

Perhaps you will not recognize them all,
nor realize how great your offering
to all the world,
when you let healing come to you.

Let yourself be healed
that you may be forgiving,
offering salvation to your brother
and yourself.

Your healing saves him pain
as well as you,
and you are healed
because you wished him well.

Your healing is the witness unto his,
and cannot be apart from his at all.

Spend but an instant in the glad acceptance
of what is given you to give your brother,
and learn with him
what has been given both of you.

And you will understand
his safety is your own,
and in his healing you are healed.

When a brother behaves insanely,
you can heal him
only by perceiving the sanity in him.

It is given you to show him, by your healing
that his guilt is but the fabric
of a senseless dream.

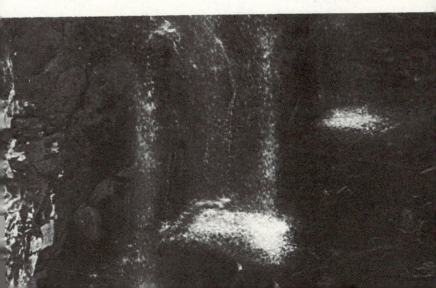

You have reached the end of an ancient journey,
not realizing yet that it is over.
You are still worn and tired,
and the desert's dust still seems
to cloud your eyes and keep you sightless.
Yet He Whom you welcomed has come to you,
and would welcome you.
He has waited long to give you this.
Receive it now of Him,
for He would have you know Him.
Only a little wall of dust
still stands between you.
Blow on it lightly and with happy laughter,
and it will fall away.
And walk into the garden
love has prepared for both of you.

Look upon your brother as yourself.
Your relationship is now a temple of healing;
a place where all the weary ones
can come and rest.

Use no relationship
to hold you to the past,
but with each one each day
be born again.
A minute, even less,
will be enough
to free you from the past.

Let us together follow in the way
that truth points out to us.
And let us be the leaders of our many brothers
who are seeking for the way, but find it not.

We go beyond the veil of fear,
lighting each other's way.
The holiness that leads us
is within us, as is our home.

2

THE DREAM OF SICKNESS

In our collective dream we take ourselves to be bodies, separate from God and from each other. The limits of the body, its sickness, suffering, and death, seem terrifyingly real and inescapable. We seem to be helpless victims of the body and world, able to enjoy fleeting pleasures for only a moment before they are snatched away again. Small wonder, then, that we live in so much fear.

This fear, says the *Course,* is both cause and effect of our dreams. It is an illusion based not on present reality, but on an imagined future. Like all illusions it is self-masking, hiding its unreality in the distortions of perception it induces. Only by looking carefully at all illusions can their distortions, unreality and lack of power over us be recognized. To look carefully at our fears and illusions is therefore to see through them. Once we see clearly, separation is recognized as "merely a faulty formulation of reality, with no effect at all." The body is seen as merely a symbol of what we thought we were, and the true function of both the world and the body is recognized as healing.

*Forgiveness is the great need of this world
but that is because it is a world of illusions.*

The Veil of Illusion

What is healing but the removal
of all that stands in the way of knowledge?
And how else can one dispel illusions
except by looking at them directly,
without protecting them?
Be not afraid, therefore,
for what you will be looking at
is the source of fear,
and you are beginning to learn
that fear is not real.

All illusions are of fear,
and they can be of nothing else.

No illusions can attract
the mind that has transcended them,
and left them far behind.

How easily do idols go
when they are still perceived
but wanted not.
How willingly the mind
can let them go
when it has understood
that idols are nothing and nowhere,
and are purposeless.

Forget not, then, that idols
must keep hidden what you are,
not from the Mind of God
but from your own.

There can be no order of difficulty in healing
merely because all sickness is illusion.

Be you thankful
that there is a place
where truth and beauty wait for you.
Go on to meet them gladly,
and learn how much awaits you
for the simple willingness
to give up nothing
because it is nothing.

There is no gap that separates
the truth from dreams
and from illusions.
Truth has left no room for them
in any place or time.
For it fills every place
and every time.

Separation Is Sickness

The world you perceive
is a world of separation.

The separation is merely
a faulty formulation of reality,
with no effect at all.

Separation is no more
than an illusion of despair.

Replace your dream of separation
with the fact of unity.
For the separation is only
the denial of union,
and correctly interpreted
attests to your eternal knowledge
that union is true.

A sick person perceives himself
as separate from God.
Would you see him as separate from you?
It is your task to heal the sense of separation
that has made him sick.
It is your function to recognize for him
that what he believes about himself
is not the truth.
It is your forgiveness
that must show him this.
Healing is very simple.

Sickness is not of the body,
but of the mind.

The acceptance of sickness
as a decision of the mind,
for a purpose for which it would use the body,
is the basis of healing.
And this is so for healing in all forms.
A patient decides that this is so,
and he recovers.
If he decides against recovery,
he will not be healed.
Who is the physician?
Only the mind of the patient himself.
The outcome is what he decides that it is.

Healing involves an understanding
of what the illusion of sickness is for.
Healing is impossible without this.

You are afraid to know God's Will,
because you believe it is not yours.
This belief is your whole sickness
and your whole fear.
Every symptom of sickness and fear
arises here,
because this is the belief
that makes you *want* not to know.
Believing this you hide in darkness,
denying that the light is in you.

The acceptance of peace
is the denial of illusion,
and sickness is an illusion.

We attend in silence and in joy.
This is the day when healing comes to us.
This is the day when separation ends,
and we remember Who we really are.

Limitations of the Body

The body is the symbol
of what you think you are.

You have made of it a symbol
for the limitations
that you want your mind
to have and see and keep.

If you use the body for attack,
it is harmful to you.
If you use it only to reach the minds
of those who believe they are bodies,
and teach them through the body
this is not so, you will understand
the power of the mind that is in you.

Sickness is anger taken out upon the body,
so that it will suffer pain.

You are not sick
and you cannot die.
But you can confuse yourself
with things that do.

"I am not a body. I am free."
It is essential for your progress in this course
that you accept today's idea,
and hold it very dear.
Be not concerned that to the ego
it is quite insane.
The ego holds the body dear
because it dwells in it,
and lives united with the home that it has made.
It is part of the illusion that has sheltered it
from being found illusory itself.

The ego uses the body for attack,
for pleasure and for pride.
The insanity of this perception
makes it a fearful one indeed.
The Holy Spirit sees the body only
as a means of communication,
and because communicating is sharing
it becomes communion.

Regard bodies solely
as a means of joining minds
and uniting them with yours and mine.
This interpretation of the body
will change your mind entirely about its value.

In the service of uniting
it becomes a beautiful lesson
in communion, which has value
until communion is.

Healing is the result of using the body
solely for communication.

To see a body as anything
except a means of communication
is to limit your mind and to hurt yourself.

You are not limited by the body. . . .
Yet mind can be manifested
through the body if it goes beyond it
and does not interpret it as limitation.
Whenever you see another
as limited to or by the body,
you are imposing this limit on yourself.
Are you willing to accept this,
when your whole purpose for learning
should be to escape from limitations?

Use it for truth and you will see it truly.
Misuse it and you will misunderstand it.

Health is the result of relinquishing
all attempts to use the body lovelessly.

Help and healing are the normal expressions
of a mind that is working through the body,
but not in it.

The mind can heal the body,
but the body cannot heal the mind.

When the body ceases to attract you,
and when you place no value on it
as a meaning of getting anything,
then there will be no interference in communication
and your thoughts will be as free as God's.

"I am not a body, I am free.
For I am still as God created me."

The World You See

This is an insane world,
and do not underestimate
the extent of its insanity.
There is no area of your perception
that it has not touched.

Learn to look upon the world
as a means of healing the separation.

Be healed that you may heal.

Your healing will extend,
and will be brought to problems
that you thought were not your own.

Healing replaces suffering.
Who looks on one cannot perceive the other,
for they cannot both be there.
And what you see the world will witness,
and will witness to.
Thus is your healing
everything the world requires,
that it may be healed.

You do not want the world.
The only thing of value in it
is whatever part of it
you look upon with love.
This gives it the only reality it will ever have.

The resurrection of the world
awaits your healing
and your happiness.

The world becomes a place of hope,
because its only purpose is to be a place
where hope of happiness can be fulfilled.
And no one stands outside this hope . . .
the purpose of the world
is one which all must share,
if hope be more than just a dream.

Come to the holy instant and be healed,
for nothing that is there received
is left behind on your returning to the world.
And being blessed you will bring blessing.
Life is given you to give the dying world.

When I am healed I am not healed alone.
And I would share my healing with the world,
that sickness may be banished from the mind
of God's one Son, who is my only Self.

Today I choose to see a world forgiven.

Time and Eternity

Healing in time is needed,
for joy cannot establish
its eternal reign
where sorrow dwells.

Accept only the function of healing in time,
because that is what time is for.

If you accept your function
in the world of time as one of healing,
you will emphasize only the aspect of time
in which healing can occur.
Healing cannot be accomplished in the past.
It must be accomplished in the present
to release the future.
This interpretation ties the future to the present,
and extends the present rather than the past.

Old ideas about time are very difficult to change,
because everything you believe is rooted in time,
and depends on your not learning
these new ideas about it.
Yet that is precisely why
you need new ideas about time.

All of time
is but the mad belief
that what is over
is still here and now.

The one wholly true thought
one can hold about the past
is that it is not here.
To think about it at all
is therefore to think about illusions.

All healing is release from the past.

There is no fantasy that does not contain
the dream of retribution for the past.
Would you act out the dream,
or let it go?

Everyone seen without the past
thus brings you nearer to the end of time
by bringing healed and healing sight
into the darkness,
and enabling the world to see.

Delay does not matter in eternity,
but it is tragic in time.
You have elected to be in time
rather than eternity, and therefore
believe you are in time.

While time lasts in your mind
there will be choices.
Time itself is your choice.
If you would remember eternity
you must look only on the eternal.
Time and eternity cannot both be real,
because they contradict each other.
If you will accept
only what is timeless as real,
you will begin to understand eternity
and make it yours.

The reflections you accept
into the mirror of your mind in time
but bring eternity nearer or farther.
But eternity itself is beyond all time.
Reach out of time and touch it,
with the help of its reflection in you.

Delay will hurt you now more than before,
only because you realize it is delay,
and that escape from pain is really possible.

If you are tempted to be dispirited
by thinking how long it would take
to change your mind so completely,
ask yourself, "How long is an instant?"

How long is an instant?
As long as it takes to reestablish
perfect sanity, perfect peace
and perfect love for everyone.

The working out of all correction
takes no time at all.
Yet the acceptance of the working out
can seem to take forever.

Now is the release from time.

The only interval in which
I can be saved from time is now.
For in this instant has forgiveness come
to set me free.

Future loss is not your fear.
But present joining is your dread.
Who can feel desolation except now?
A future cause as yet has no effects.
And therefore must it be that if you fear,
there is a present cause.
And it is this that needs correction,
not a future state.

You are but asked to let the future go,
and place it in God's Hands.
And you will see by your experience
that you have laid the past and present
in His Hands as well,
because the past will punish you no more,
and future dread will now be meaningless.
Release the future.
For the past is gone,
and what is present,
freed from its bequest
of grief and misery,
of pain and loss,
becomes the instant in which time
escapes the bondage of illusions
where it runs its pitiless, inevitable course.
Then is each instant which was slave to time
transformed into a holy instant,
when the light that was kept hidden in God's Son
is freed to bless the world.
Now is he free, and all his glory
shines upon a world made free with him,
to share his holiness.

Place, then, your future in the Hands of God.
For thus you call the memory of Him to come again,
replacing all your thoughts of sin and evil
with the truth of love.
Think you the world could fail to gain thereby,
and every living creature not respond
with healed perception?
Who entrusts himself to God
has also placed the world within the Hands
to which he has himself appealed
for comfort and security.
He lays aside the sick illusions of the world
along with his
and offers peace to both.

"*I place the future in the Hands of God.*"

From Fear to Faith

Healing is a way of forgetting
the sense of danger
the ego has induced in you,
by not recognizing its existence
in your brother.

Fear is a symptom
of your own deep sense of loss.
If when you perceive it in others
you learn to supply the loss,
the basic cause of fear is removed.
Thereby you teach yourself
that fear does not exist in you.
The means for removing it is in yourself
and you have demonstrated this by giving it.

Fear cannot long be hidden by illusions,
for it is part of them.
It will escape and take another form,
being the source of all illusions.

You must remember, however,
that the *Course* states, and repeatedly,
that its purpose is the escape from fear.

You too will laugh at your fears
and replace them with peace.
For fear lies not in reality,
but in the minds of children
who do not understand reality.
It is only their lack of understanding
that frightens them,
and when they learn to perceive truly
they are not afraid.

The more you look at fear the less you see it,
and the clearer what it conceals becomes.

Very simply, then,
you may believe you are afraid of nothingness,
but you are really afraid of nothing.
And in that awareness you are healed.

The "fearful healer"
is a contradiction in terms.

An individual may ask for physical healing
because he is fearful of bodily harm.
At the same time,
if he were healed physically,
the threat to his thought system
might be considerably more fearful to him
than its physical expression.
In this case he is not really asking
for release from fear,
but for the removal of a symptom
that he himself selected.
This request is, therefore, not for healing at all.

Fear does not gladden.
Healing does.
Fear always makes exceptions.
Healing never does.
Fear produces dissociation,
because it induces separation.
Healing always produces harmony,
because it proceeds from integration.

Give faith to one another
for faith and hope and mercy
are yours to give.
Into the hands that give, the gift is given.

By faith, you offer the gift
of freedom from the past.

Realize that there is nothing
faith cannot forgive.
No error interferes
with its calm sight.

To have faith is to heal.

All fear is past
because its source is gone,
and all its thoughts gone with it.
Love remains the only present state.

3

The Causes of
the Dream

Our dream, says the *Course,* is a dream of attack and vengeance. We attack ourselves and one another for our imagined sins, while in reality our Self remains untouched by such illusions. Yet because we take the dream to be reality, its effects seem equally real. Our imagined attacks create fear, guilt, and anger, which seem to justify further attack. Thus a vicious cycle is set up and the dream is perpetuated.

Only by changing our minds, the source of both the cause and cure of the dream, can we hope to awaken. We must learn to shift our perception from a focus on mistakes, our own and those of others, to a focus on the underlying love and innocence that are our true nature. To the extent that we do this, we will realize that anger, attack, and guilt are unjustified, and our dream of vengeance will be recognized for the illusion that it is.

You are the dreamer
of the world of dreams.

Attack and Blame

There is nothing to prevent you
from recognizing all calls for help
as exactly what they are,
except your own imagined
need to attack.
It is only this
that makes you willing to engage
in endless "battles" with reality
in which you deny the reality
of the need for healing
by making it unreal.
You would not do this
except for your unwillingness
to accept reality as it is.

It is when judgment ceases
that healing occurs.

We are restored to sanity,
in which we understand
that anger is insane, attack is mad,
and vengeance merely foolish fantasy.

The response of holiness
to any form of error
is always the same.
There is no contradiction
in what holiness calls forth.
Its one response is healing.

As blame is withdrawn from without,
there is a strong tendency
to harbor it within.
It is difficult at first to realize
that this is exactly the same thing,
for there is no distinction
between within and without.

If your brothers are part of you
and you blame them for your deprivation,
you are blaming yourself.
And you cannot blame yourself
without blaming them.
That is why blame must be undone,
not seen elsewhere.
Lay it to yourself
and you cannot know yourself,
for only the ego blames at all.
Self-blame is therefore ego identification,
and as much an ego defense
as blaming others.

Come wholly without condemnation,
for otherwise you will believe
that the door is barred
and you cannot enter.
The door is not barred,
and it is impossible that you cannot enter
the place where God would have you be.

Escape from Guilt

Relieve the mind
of the insane burden of guilt
it carries so wearily,
and healing is accomplished.

You are whole only in your guiltlessness,
and only in your guiltlessness
can you be happy.

Guiltlessness is invulnerability.

As long as you feel guilty
you are listening to the voice of the ego.

When you maintain that you are guilty
but the source of your guilt lies in the past,
you are not looking inward.
The past is not in you.
Your weird associations to it
have no meaning in the present.
Yet you let them stand
between you and your brothers,
with whom you find
no real relationships at all.

No real relationship can rest on guilt.

Who is there but wishes to be free of pain?
He may not yet have learned
how to exchange guilt for innocence,
nor realize that only in this exchange
can freedom from pain be his.
Yet those who have failed to learn
need teaching, not attack.

The end of guilt
is in your hands to give.
Would you stop now
to look for guilt in one another?

You restore guiltlessness
to whomever you see as guiltless.

From everyone whom you accord
release from guilt
you will inevitably learn your innocence.

In the crystal cleanness
of the release you give
is your instantaneous escape from guilt.

All salvation is escape from guilt.

The Power of Perception

Do you not see that all your misery
comes from the strange belief
that you are powerless?

Uncorrected error of any kind
deceives you about the power
that is in you to make correction.

You see what you expect,
and you expect what you invite.
Your perception is the result of your invitation,
coming to you as you sent for it.

The value of deciding in advance
what you want to happen
is simply that you will perceive the situation
as a means to make it happen.
You will therefore make every effort
to overlook what interferes
with the accomplishment of your objective.

Perception has a focus.
It is this that gives consistency
to what you see.
Change but this focus,
and what you behold will change accordingly.
Your vision now will shift,
to give support to the intent
which has replaced the one you held before.

It is still up to you
to choose to join with truth
or with illusion.
But remember that to choose one
is to let the other go.
Which one you choose
you will endow with beauty and reality,
because the choice depends
on which you value more.
The spark of beauty
or the veil of ugliness,
the real world
or the world of guilt and fear,
truth or illusion,
freedom or slavery.

The power to heal the Son of God is given you
because he must be one with you.
You are responsible for how he sees himself.
And reason tells you it is given you
to change his whole mind,
which is one with you,
in just an instant.
And any instant serves
to bring complete correction of his errors
and make him whole.
The instant that you choose
to let yourself be healed,
in that same instant is his whole salvation
seen as complete with yours.

The miracle is a lesson
in total perception.

To heal, then, is to correct perception
in your brother and yourself.

The reestablishing of meaning
in a chaotic thought system
is the way to heal it.

It is but your thoughts
that bring you fear,
and your deliverance
depends on you.

What I see reflects a process in my mind,
which starts with my idea of what I want.

I can be hurt
by nothing but my thoughts.

We practice coming nearer
to the light in us today.
We take our wandering thoughts,
and gently bring them back
to where they fall in line
with all the thoughts we share with God.
We will not let them stray.
We let the light within our minds
direct them to come home.

I can elect to change
all thoughts that hurt.
And I would go beyond these words today,
and past all reservations,
and arrive at full acceptance
of the truth in them.

Learning and Teaching

The essential thing is learning
that you do not know.

Those who remember always
that they know nothing,
and who have become willing
to learn everything, will learn it.

Trials are but lessons
that you failed to learn
presented once again,
so where you made a faulty choice before
you now can make a better one,
and thus escape all pain
that what you chose before has brought to you.

Healing thus becomes
a lesson in understanding,
and the more you practice it
the better teacher and learner you become.

You can learn to bless,
and cannot give what you have not.
If, then, you offer blessing,
it must have come first to yourself.
And you must also have accepted it as yours,
for how else could you give it away?

If you have denied truth,
what better witnesses
to its reality could you have
than those who have been healed by it?
But be sure to count yourself among them,
for in your willingness to join them
is your healing accomplished.

All things are lessons
God would have me learn.

Today I learn to give
as I receive.

What you made has imprisoned your will,
and given you a sick mind
that must be healed.
Your vigilance against this sickness
is the way to heal it.
Once your mind is healed it radiates health,
and thereby teaches healing.
This establishes you as a teacher.

Teaching is done in many ways,
above all by example.
Teaching should be healing,
because it is the sharing
of ideas.

When a teacher of God fails to heal,
it is because he has forgotten Who he is.

In order to heal,
it thus becomes essential
for the teacher of God
to let all his own mistakes be corrected.

Teach only love,
for that is what you are.

A Change of Mind

Anyone is free to change his mind,
and all his thoughts change with it.
Now the source of thought has shifted,
for to change your mind
means you have changed the source
of all ideas you think or ever thought
or yet will think.
You free the past from what you thought before.
You free the future from all ancient thoughts
of seeking what you do not want to find.

There can be nothing
that a change of mind cannot affect,
for all external things are only shadows
of a decision already made.
Change the decision,
and how can its shadow be unchanged?

Sickness is of the mind,
and has nothing to do with the body.
What does this recognition "cost"?
It costs the whole world you see,
for the world will never again
appear to rule the mind.
For with this recognition
is responsibility placed where it belongs;
not with the world,
but on him who looks on the world
and sees it as it is not.
He looks on what he chooses to see.
No more and no less.
The world does nothing to him.
He only thought it did.
Nor does he do anything to the world,
because he was mistaken about what it is.
Herein is the release
from guilt and sickness both,
for they are one.

Knowledge cannot dawn on a mind
full of illusions,
because truth and illusions
are irreconcilable.
Truth is whole,
and cannot be known
by part of a mind.

All forms of sickness
are signs that the mind is split,
and does not accept
a unified purpose.

When you limit yourself
we are not of one mind,
and that is sickness.

The miracle comes quietly
into the mind that stops an instant and is still.
It reaches gently from that quiet time,
and from the mind it healed in quiet then,
to other minds to share its quietness.
And they will join in doing nothing
to prevent its radiant extension
back into the Mind Which caused all minds to be.
Born out of sharing,
there can be no pause in time
to cause the miracle delay
in hastening to all unquiet minds,
and bringing them an instant's stillness,
when the memory of God returns to them.

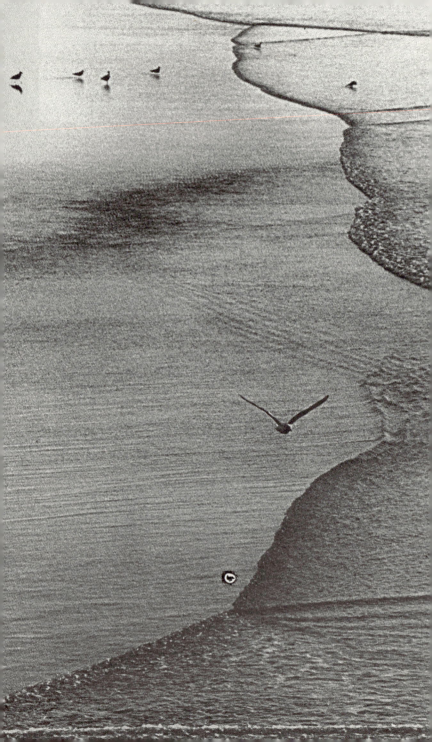

The power of one mind
can shine into another,
because all the lamps of God
were lit by the same spark.
It is everywhere
and it is eternal.

Your mind is so powerful a light
that you can look into theirs
and enlighten them,
as I can enlighten yours.
I want to share my mind with you
because we are of one Mind,
and that Mind is ours.
See only this Mind everywhere,
because only this is everywhere
and in everything.
It is everything
because it encompasses
all things within itself.
Blessed are you who perceive only this,
because you perceive only what is true.

When a mind has only light,
it knows only light.
Its own radiance shines all around it,
and extends out into the darkness
of other minds,
transforming them into majesty.

The mind that is made willing
to accept God's gifts
has been restored to spirit,
and extends its freedom and its joy.

4

THE MEANS OF AWAKENING

To awaken from our dream of pain and suffering, we must first recognize that we are dreaming. Only then will we see that dreaming is our choice, that we can create dreams of happiness instead of pain, and that we can ultimately awaken from all dreams. Because the dreams of this world are so filled with fear, the *Course* says that it is very difficult for us to view even reality and awakening without fear. Therefore, instead of hurling us abruptly into reality while we still dread it, the *Course* offers a gentle progressive change of mind in which our dreams of fear are changed to dreams of happiness, our dreams of anger and attack to dreams of gratitude and forgiveness.

These happy dreams reflect reality and our natural state, which are loving and joyous. This shift in perception from fear to love is what is called a *miracle*. It shows us that we are the creators of our dreams and it points beyond all dreams to awakening.

The *Course* focuses on healing relationships as a means of mutual awakening. These relationships may occur spontaneously, but sometimes a formal psychotherapeutic relationship can also be helpful. Relationship is central to the healing process and whether in therapy or not, we are both patient and therapist, student and teacher for each other.

> *Healing is release from the fear of waking*
> *and the substitution of the decision to wake.*

Awakening from the Dream

The dreamer of a dream is not awake,
but does not know he sleeps.
He sees illusions of himself
as sick or well, depressed or happy.

What is done in dreams
has not really been done.
It is impossible to convince
the dreamer that this is so,
for dreams are what they are
because of their illusion of reality.
Only in waking is the full release from them,
for only then does it become perfectly apparent
that they had no effect upon reality at all,
and did not change it.

Yet if you are the dreamer,
you perceive this much at least:
That you have caused the dream,
and can accept another dream as well.
But for this change in content in the dream,
it must be realized that it is you
who dreamed the dreaming that you do not like.
It is but an effect that you have caused.

Nothing at all has happened
but that you have put yourself to sleep,
and dreamed a dream
in which you were alien to yourself,
and but a part of someone else's dream.
The miracle does not awaken you,
but merely shows you who the dreamer is.
It teaches you there is a choice of dreams
while you are still asleep,
depending on the purpose of your dreaming.
Do you wish for dreams of healing,
or for dreams of death?

A dream is like a memory
in that it pictures
what you wanted shown to you.

The dreams forgiveness lets the mind perceive
do not induce another form of sleep,
so that the dreamer dreams another dream.
His happy dreams are heralds of the dawn
of truth upon the mind.
They lead from sleep to gentle waking,
so that dreams are gone.

In forgiving dreams is no one asked
to be the victim and the sufferer.
These are the happy dreams.

This world is full of miracles.
They stand in shining silence
next to every dream of pain and suffering,
of sin and guilt.
They are the dream's alternative,
the choice to be the dreamer,
rather than deny the active role
in making up the dream.

When you accept a miracle,
you do not add your dream of fear
to one that is already being dreamed.
Without support, the dream will fade away
without effects.
For it is your support that strengthens it.

Healing might thus be called a counter-dream,
which cancels out the dream of sickness
in the name of truth.

The mind which understands that sickness
can be nothing but a dream
is not deceived by forms the dream may take.
Sickness where guilt is absent cannot come,
for it is but another form of guilt.
Atonement does not heal the sick,
for that is not a cure.
It takes away the guilt
that makes the sickness possible.
And that is cure indeed.

"Cure" is a word that cannot be applied
to any remedy the world accepts as beneficial.
What the world perceives as therapeutic
is but what will make the body "better."
When it tries to heal the mind,
it sees no separation from the body,
where it thinks the mind exists.
Its forms of healing thus must substitute
illusion for illusion.
One belief in sickness takes another form,
and so the patient now perceives himself as well.

He is not healed.
He merely had a dream that he was sick,
and in the dream he found a magic formula
to make him well.
Yet he has not awakened from the dream,
and so his mind remains exactly as it was before.
He has not seen the light
that would awaken him and end the dream.
What difference does the content
of a dream make in reality?
One either sleeps or wakens.
There is nothing in between.

You must learn the cost of sleeping,
and refuse to pay it.
Only then will you decide to awaken.

Healing is release from the fear of waking
and the substitution of the decision to wake.

Healing is freedom.
For it demonstrates that dreams
will not prevail against the truth.

Who would put his faith in dreams
once they are recognized for what they are?
Awareness of dreaming
is the real function of God's teachers.
They watch the dream figures come and go,
shift and change, suffer and die.
Yet they are not deceived by what they see.
They recognize that to behold a dream figure
as sick and separate is no more real
than to regard it as healthy and beautiful.
Unity alone is not a thing of dreams.
And it is this God's teachers acknowledge
as behind the dream, beyond all seeming
and yet surely theirs.

Looking Within

Healing does not come
from anyone else.
You must accept guidance
from within.

No one who comes here
but must still have hope,
some lingering illusion,
or some dream that there is something
outside of himself
that will bring happiness and peace to him.
If everything is in him
this cannot be so.

Seek not outside yourself.
For all your pain
comes simply from a futile search
for what you want,
insisting where it must be found.
What if it is not there?
Do you prefer that you be right or happy?
Be you glad that you are told
where happiness abides,
and seek no longer elsewhere.
You will fail.
But it is given you to know the truth,
and not to seek for it outside yourself.

Heal and be healed.
There is no other choice of pathways
that can ever lead to peace.

There is a sense of peace so deep
that no dream in this world
has ever brought even a dim imagining
of what it is.

Peace be to you to whom is healing offered.
And you will learn that peace is given you
when you accept the healing for yourself.
What occurred within the instant
that love entered in without attack
will stay forever.
Your healing will be one of its effects.

Brother, the war against yourself is almost over.
The journey's end is at the place of peace.
Would you not now accept
the peace offered you here?

Health is inner peace.

To have peace, teach peace.

Limit the peace you share,
and your Self must be unknown to you.

The purpose of your learning
is to enable you
to bring the quiet with you,
and to heal distress and turmoil.
This is not done by avoiding them
and seeking a haven of isolation
for yourself.

We who are one
would recognize this day
the truth about ourselves.
We would come home, and rest in unity.
For there is peace, and nowhere else
can peace be sought and found.

When peace comes at last
to those who wrestle with temptation
and fight against the giving in to sin;
when the light comes at last into the mind
given to contemplation;
or when the goal is finally achieved by anyone,
it always comes with just one happy realization;
"I need do nothing."

Psychotherapy

Psychotherapy is the only form of therapy there is.
Since only the mind can be sick,
only the mind can be healed.
Only the mind is in need of healing.
This does not appear to be the case,
for the manifestations of this world
seem real indeed.
Psychotherapy is necessary so that an individual
can begin to question their reality.
Sometimes he is able to start
to open his mind without formal help,
but even then it is always some change
in his perception of interpersonal relationships
that enables him to do so.
Sometimes he needs a more structured,
extended relationship with an "official" therapist.
Either way, the task is the same;
the patient must be helped to change his mind
about the "reality" of illusions.

Very simply, the purpose of psychotherapy
is to remove the blocks to truth.

Illness of any kind may be defined
as the result of a view of the self
as weak, vulnerable, evil and endangered,
and thus in need of constant defense.

Psychotherapy is a process
that changes the view of the self.

Psychotherapy, correctly understood,
teaches forgiveness and helps the patient
to recognize and accept it.

A therapist does not heal;
he lets healing be.

Who, then, is the therapist,
and who is the patient?
In the end everyone is both.
He who needs healing must heal.

Everyone is both patient and therapist
in every relationship in which he enters.

Forgiveness and Gratitude

To forgive is to heal.

Forgiveness removes only the untrue,
lifting the shadows from the world
and carrying it, safe and sure
within its gentleness.

Forgive all thoughts
which would oppose the truth
of your completion, unity and peace.

What is forgiveness
but a willingness that truth be true?
What can remain unhealed
and broken from a Unity
which holds all things within itself?

All that stood between your image of yourself
and what you are,
forgiveness washes joyfully away.

Pardon is always justified.
It has a sure foundation.

Forgiveness recognized as merited
will heal.

Do not forget today
that there can be no form of suffering
that fails to hide an unforgiving thought.
Nor can there be a form of pain
forgiveness cannot heal.

True forgiveness . . .
must heal the mind that gives,
for giving is receiving.

Rejoice in the power of forgiveness
to heal your sight completely.

Without the darkness of the past upon your eyes,
you cannot fail to see today.
And what you see will be so welcome
that you will gladly extend today forever.

In complete forgiveness,
in which you recognize
that there is nothing to forgive,
you are absolved completely.

Be glad indeed salvation asks so little,
not so much.
It asks for nothing in reality.
And even in illusions it but asks
forgiveness be the substitute for fear.

Those who have been forgiven
must devote themselves first to healing
because having received the idea of healing,
they must give it to hold it.

You understand that you are healed
when you give healing.
You accept forgiveness
as accomplished in yourself
when you forgive.
You recognize your brother as yourself,
and thus do you perceive
that you are whole.

Forgiveness is a choice.
I never see my brother as he is,
for that is far beyond perception.
What I see in him
is merely what I wish to see
because it stands for what
I want to be the truth.
It is to this alone that I respond,
however much I seem to be
impelled by outside happenings.

Look on your brother with the willingness
to see him as he is.
And do not keep a part of him
outside your willingness that he be healed.
To heal is to make whole.
And what is whole can have no missing parts
that have been kept outside.
Forgiveness rests on recognizing this.

In your forgiveness of this stranger,
alien to you and yet your ancient Friend,
lies his release and your redemption with him.

Think not that your forgiveness of your brother
serves but you two alone.
For the whole new world rests in the hands
of every two who enter here to rest.

Today we learn to think of gratitude
in place of anger, malice and revenge.
We have been given everything.
If we refuse to recognize it,
we are not entitled therefore to our bitterness,
and to a self-perception which regards
us in a place of merciless pursuit,
where we are badgered ceaselessly,
and pushed about without a thought or care
for us or for our future.
Gratitude becomes the single thought
we substitute for these insane perceptions.

Walk, then, in gratitude
the way of love.
For hatred is forgotten
when we lay comparisons aside.
What more remains
as obstacles to peace?

Then let our brothers
lean their tired heads
against our shoulders
as they rest awhile.
We offer thanks for them.
For if we can direct them
to the peace that we would find,
the way is opening at last to us.

When your forgiveness is complete
you will have total gratitude.

Forgiveness is the means
by which I will recognize my innocence.

My forgiveness is the means
by which the world is healed,
together with myself.
Let me, then, forgive the world,
that it may be healed along with me.

Reality and Truth

Reality is here.
It belongs to you and me and God,
and is perfectly satisfying to all of us.
Only this awareness heals,
because it is the awareness of truth.

Reality can dawn only on an unclouded mind.
It is always there to be accepted,
but its acceptance depends
on your willingness to have it.

What can be fearful but fantasy,
and who turns to fantasy unless he despairs
of finding satisfaction in reality?

You need reality to dispel your fears.
Would you not exchange your fears for truth,
if the exchange is yours for the asking?

Appearances deceive, but can be changed.
Reality is changeless. It does not deceive at all,
and if you fail to see beyond appearances
you are deceived.

We go beyond appearances today
and reach the source of healing.

Remember that you always choose
between truth and illusion.

So healing must replace
the fantasies of sickness.

Truth cannot fail to heal and heal forever.

Do not defend yourself
against the truth.

Let truth be what it is.
Do not intrude upon it,
do not attack it,
do not interrupt its coming.
Let it encompass every situation
and bring you peace.
Not even faith is asked of you,
for truth asks nothing.
Let it enter,
and it will call forth and secure for you
the faith you need for peace.

When truth has come
it harbors in its wings
the gift of perfect constancy,
and love which does not falter
in the face of pain.

When truth has come all pain is over,
for there is no room for transitory thoughts
and dead ideas to linger in your mind.
Truth occupies your mind completely,
liberating you from all beliefs in the ephemeral.
They have no place because the truth has come,
and they are nowhere.
They cannot be found,
for truth is everywhere forever, now.

Healing will flash across your open mind,
as peace and truth arise
to take the place of war
and vain imaginings.

To be healed is merely to accept
what has always been the simple truth,
and always will remain
exactly as it has forever been.

To believe in truth
you do not have to do anything.

We are concerned only
with giving welcome to the truth.

Truth merely wants to give you happiness,
for such its purpose is.

The truth of what we are
is not for words to speak of nor describe.
Yet we can realize our function here,
and words can speak of this and teach it, too,
if we exemplify the words in us.

Do not be confused about what must be healed,
but tell yourself:

"I have forgotten what I really am.
For I mistook my body for myself."

Ask the truth to come to us
and set us free.
And truth will come,
for it has never been apart from us.
It merely waits for just this invitation
which we give today.
We introduce it with a healing prayer,
to help us rise above defensiveness,
and let truth be as it has always been:

"Sickness is a defense against the truth.
I will accept the truth of what I am,
And let my mind be wholly healed today."

5

THE JOY OF FREEDOM

The end of dreaming brings an end to fear and pain.
With awakening, says the *Course,* comes the love, light,
peace, and joy of freedom. Even before complete awakening, we receive glimpses of this state. These glimpses
come through what *A Course in Miracles* calls *vision* and
a holy instant. A holy instant is one in which we directly
experience our true nature and reality. Vision is the
inner seeing that pictures this reality to us. The *Course*
emphasizes that the holy instant and vision have enor-
mous healing power, both for ourselves and for others,
because reality itself is healing. But reality offers more
than healing: in it we are filled with love, peace, and joy
beyond our wildest dreams. For ultimately we are beyond all dreams, and the end of dreaming is a gift of
healing.

To love yourself
is to heal yourself.

The Holy Instant

The holy instant
is this instant
and every instant.

The holy instant is eternal,
and your illusions of time
will not prevent the timeless
from being what it is,
nor you from experiencing it as it is.

What is the holy instant
but God's appeal to you
to recognize what He has given you?
Here is the great appeal to reason;
the awareness of what is always there to see,
the happiness that could be always yours.
Here is the constant peace
you could experience forever.

The instant of holiness is shared,
and cannot be yours alone.
Remember, then, when you are tempted
to attack a brother,
that his instant of release is yours.
Miracles are the instants of release you offer,
and will receive.

Forget not that your relationship is one,
and so it must be
that whatever threatens the peace of one
is an equal threat to the other.
The power of joining its blessing lies in the fact
that it is now impossible for you or your brother
to experience fear alone,
or to attempt to deal with it alone.

Never believe that this is necessary,
or even possible.
Yet just as this is impossible,
so is it equally impossible
that the holy instant come to either of you
without the other.
And it will come to both
at the request of either.

Whoever is saner at the time
[a] threat is perceived should remember
how deep is his indebtedness to the other
and how much gratitude is due him,
and be glad that he can pay his debt
by bringing happiness to both.
Let him remember this, and say:

    "I desire this holy instant for myself,
    that I may share it with my brother,
    whom I love.
    It is not possible
    that I can have it without him,
    or he without me.
    Yet it is wholly possible
    for us to share it now.
    And so I choose this instant
    as the one to offer to the Holy Spirit,
    that His blessing may descend on us,
    and keep us both in peace."

And may the holy instant
speed you on the way,
as it will surely do
if you but let it come to you.

Vision and Wholeness

Vision will correct the perception
of everything you see.

Everything looked upon with vision
is healed and holy.

Recognizing that what I see
reflects what I think I am,
I realize that vision is my greatest need.
The world I see attests to the fearful nature
of the self-image I have made.
If I would remember who I am,
it is essential
that I let this image of myself go.
As it is replaced by truth,
vision will surely be given me.
And with this vision,
I will look upon the world
and on myself
with charity and love.

Vision will come to you
at first in glimpses,
but they will be enough
to show you what is given you
who see your brother sinless.

Forget not that the choice
of sin or truth, helplessness or power,
is the choice of whether to attack or heal.
For healing comes of power
and attack of helplessness.
Whom you attack you cannot want to heal.
And whom you would have healed
must be the one you chose
to be protected from attack.

And what is this decision but the choice
whether to see him through the body's eyes,
or let him be revealed to you through vision?
How this decision leads to its effects
is not your problem.
But what you want to see
must be your choice.

To your tired eyes I bring a vision
of a different world,
so new and clean and fresh
you will forget the pain and sorrow
that you saw before.
Yet this a vision is
which you must share
with everyone you see,
for otherwise you will behold it not.
To give this gift is how to make it yours.

Vision, being healed, has power to heal.
This is the light that brings
your peace of mind to other minds,
to share it and be glad
that they are one with you
and with themselves.
This is the light that heals.

Everything looked upon with vision
falls gently into place.

Vision sets all things right,
bringing them gently
within the kindly sway
of Heaven's laws.

Vision is the means by which the Holy Spirit
translates your nightmares into happy dreams;
your wild hallucinations that show you
all the fearful outcomes of imagined sin
into the calm and reassuring sights
with which He would replace them.
These gentle sights and sounds
are looked on happily, and heard with joy.

Hallucinations disappear
when they are recognized for what they are.
This is the healing and the remedy.
Believe them not and they are gone.
And all you need to do is recognize
that you did this.
Once you accept this simple fact
and take into yourself the power you gave them,
you are released from them.

You have the vision now
to look past all illusions.

Your vision has become the greatest power
for the undoing of illusion
that God Himself could give.

Let us lift up our eyes together,
not in fear but faith.
And there will be no fear in us,
for in our vision will be no illusions;
only a pathway to the open door of Heaven,
the home we share in quietness
and where we live in gentleness and peace,
as one together.

There is no problem, no event or situation,
no perplexity that vision will not solve.
All is redeemed when looked upon with vision.

Christ's vision has one law.
It does not look upon a body,
and mistake it for the Son whom God created.
It beholds a light beyond the body;
an idea beyond what can be touched,
a purity undimmed by errors, pitiful mistakes,
and fearful thoughts of guilt from dreams of sin.
It sees no separation.
And it looks on everyone,
on every circumstance, all happenings
and all events,
without the slightest fading
of the light it sees.

This can be taught; and must be taught
by all who would achieve it.
It requires but the recognition
that the world cannot give anything
that faintly can compare with this in value;
nor set up a goal that does not merely disappear
when this has been perceived.

What is a miracle but this remembering?

Child of peace, the light has come to you.
The light you bring you do not recognize,
and yet you will remember.
Who can deny himself the vision
that he brings to others?

Healing is a sign
that you want to make whole.

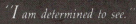
"I am determined to see."

Those whom you heal
bear witness to your healing,
for in their wholeness
you will see your own.

Sanity is wholeness,
and the sanity of your brothers
is yours.

To be wholehearted you must be happy.
If fear and love cannot coexist,
and if it is impossible to be wholly fearful
and remain alive,
the only possible whole state
is the wholly joyous.
To heal or to make joyous
is therefore the same as to integrate
and to make one.

Our minds are whole
because they are one.

By healing you learn of wholeness,
and by learning of wholeness
you learn to remember God.

Completion lies first in union,
and then in the extension of union.

Christ waits for your acceptance
of Him as yourself,
and of His Wholeness
as yours.

The wholeness of God,
which is His peace,
cannot be appreciated
except by a whole mind
that recognizes the wholeness
of God's creation.

Beyond the body, beyond the sun and stars,
past everything you see and yet somehow familiar,
is an arc of golden light
that stretches as you look
into a great and shining circle.
And all the circle fills with light
before your eyes.
The edges of the circle disappear,
and what is in it is no longer contained at all.
The light expands and covers everything,
extending to infinity forever shining
and with no break or limit anywhere.
Within it everything is joined
in perfect continuity.
Nor is it possible to imagine
that anything could be outside,
for there is nowhere
that this light is not.

Here is the meaning of what you are;
a part of this with all of it within,
and joined to all as all is joined in you.
Accept the vision that can show you this.

The Atonement is not the price
of your wholeness,
but it is the price
of your awareness of your wholeness.

The Atonement is but the way back
to what was never lost.

The purpose of Atonement
is to dispel illusions,
not to establish them as real
and then forgive them.

Accept Atonement and you are healed.

Between the future and the past
the laws of God must intervene,
if you would free yourself.
Atonement stands between them
like a lamp shining so brightly
that the chain of darkness
in which you bound yourself
will disappear.

You do not know your joy
because you do not know
your own Self-fullness.
Exclude any part of the Kingdom from yourself
and you are not whole.
A split mind cannot perceive its fullness,
and needs the miracle of its wholeness
to dawn upon it and heal it.
This reawakens the wholeness in it.

Your Self-fullness is as boundless as God's.
Like His, It extends forever
and in perfect peace.
Its radiance is so intense
that It creates in perfect joy,
and only the whole
can be born of Its wholeness.

Love and Joy

Lay forgiveness on your mind
and let all fear be gently laid aside,
that love may find its rightful place in you.

Perceive in sickness
but another call for love,
and offer your brother
what he believes
he cannot offer himself.

If you would look upon love,
which is the world's reality,
how could you do better than to recognize,
in every defense against it,
the underlying appeal for it?
And how could you better learn of its reality
than by answering the appeal for it
by giving it?

Understanding brings appreciation
and appreciation brings love.

Exempt no one from your love,
or you will be hiding a dark place in your mind
where the Holy Spirit is not welcome.
And thus you will exempt yourself
from His healing power,
for by not offering total love
you will not be healed completely.

When you want only love
you will see nothing else.

What occurred within the instant
that love entered in without attack
will stay forever.
Your healing will be one of its effects.

You will identify
with what you think will make you safe.
Whatever it may be,
you will believe that it is one with you.
Your safety lies in truth, and not in lies.
Love is your safety.
Fear does not exist.
Identify with love, and you are safe.
Identify with love, and you are home.
Identify with love, and find your Self.

Love is your power.

Brother we heal together
as we live together
and love together.

Healing is a thought
by which two minds
perceive their oneness
and become glad.

You are sad
because you are not fulfilling your function
as co-creator with God,
and are therefore depriving yourself of joy.

To heal is to make happy.
I have told you to think
how many opportunities you have had
to gladden yourself,
and how many you have refused.
This is the same as telling you
that you have refused to heal yourself.

Think of this awhile:
The world you see does nothing.
It has no effects at all.
It merely represents your thoughts.
And it will change entirely
as you elect to change your mind,
and choose the joy of God
as what you really want.
Your Self is radiant in this holy joy,
unchanged, unchanging and unchangeable
forever and forever.

The light that belongs to you
is the light of joy.
Radiance is not associated with sorrow.
Joy calls forth
an integrated willingness to share it,
and promotes the mind's natural impulse
to respond as one.
Those who attempt to heal
without being wholly joyous themselves
call forth different kinds of responses
at the same time,
and thus deprive others
of the joy of responding wholeheartedly.

Joy is unified purpose.

Joy and peace are not but idle dreams.
They are your right,
because of what you are.

Truth replaces fear,
and joy becomes what you expect
to take the place of pain.

Will you not answer
the call of love with joy?

Only the healed mind
can experience revelation
with lasting effect,
because revelation is an experience
of pure joy.

Only joy increases forever,
since joy and eternity are inseparable.

We are free to choose our joy instead of pain,
our holiness in place of sin,
the peace of God instead of conflict,
and the light of Heaven
for the darkness of the world.

The Light in You

There is a light that this world cannot give.
Yet you can give it, as it was given you.
And as you give it, it shines forth
to call you from the world and follow it.
For this light will attract you
as nothing in this world can do.

Ask for light
and learn that you are light.

Sit quietly and close your eyes.
The light within you is sufficient.
It alone has power
to give the gift of sight to you.
Exclude the outer world,
and let your thoughts fly
to the peace within.
They know the way.

In shining peace within you
is the perfect purity
in which you were created.
Fear not to look upon the lovely truth in you.
Look past darkness to the holy place
where you will see the light.

Shining purity,
wholly untouched by guilt
and wholly loving,
is bright within you.

Light is unlimited,
and spreads across this world
in quiet joy.

Only you can deprive yourself of anything.
Do not oppose this realization,
for it is truly the beginning
of the dawn of light.
Remember also that the denial
of this simple fact takes many forms,
and these you must learn to recognize
and to oppose steadfastly, without exception.
This is a crucial step in the reawakening.

The past can cast no shadow
to darken the present,
unless you are afraid of the light.
And only if you are would you choose
to bring darkness with you,
and by holding it in your mind,
see it as a dark cloud
that shrouds your brothers
and conceals their reality from your sight.

Dreams disappear
when light has come
and you can see.

Alone we are all lowly,
but together we shine
with brightness so intense
that none of us alone
can even think of it.

Each one you see in light
brings your light closer to your awareness.

Behold your brothers in their freedom,
and learn from them how to be free of darkness.
The light in you will waken them,
and they will not leave you asleep.

The lamp is lit in both of you for one another.
And by the hands that gave it to your brother
shall both of you be led past fear to love.

Every chance given him to heal
is another opportunity
to replace darkness with light
and fear with love.
If he refuses it he binds himself to darkness,
because he did not choose to free his brother
and enter light with him.

All those you brought with you
will shine on you,
and you will shine on them in gratitude
because they brought you here.
Your light will join with theirs
in power so compelling,
that it will draw the others out of darkness
as you look on them.

The light in one awakens it in all.
And when you see it in your brother,
you are remembering for everyone.

The light that joins you
shines throughout the universe,
and because it joins you,
so it makes you one with your Creator.

Rest in God

When you heal,
you are remembering the laws of God
and forgetting the laws of the ego.

Healing, then,
is a way of approaching knowledge
by thinking in accordance
with the laws of God,
and recognizing their universality.

Where two have joined for healing,
God is there.

Everyone is equally entitled to His gift
of healing and deliverance and peace.

No one can lose and everyone must gain
whenever any gift of God
has been requested and received by anyone.

Be not restless,
for you undertake a quiet journey
to the peace of God.

"I rest in God."
Completely undismayed,
this thought will carry you
through storms and strife
past misery and pain, past loss and death,
and onward to the certainty of God.
There is no suffering it cannot heal.
There is no problem that it cannot solve.
And no appearance but will turn to truth
before the eyes of you who rest in God.

This is the day of peace.
You rest in God,
and while the world is torn by winds of hate
your rest remains completely undisturbed.
Yours is the rest of truth.

As you close your eyes,
sink into stillness.
Let these periods of rest and respite
reassure your mind
that all its frantic fantasies
were but the dreams of fever
that has passed away.
Let it be still
and thankfully accept its healing.
No more fearful dreams will come,
now that you rest in God.

REFERENCES

To facilitate further study, we have referenced each passage included in this book, citing the volume and page number from which it was excerpted. WB stands for Workbook, T for Text, MT for Manual for Teachers and P for Psychotherapy. A Course in Miracles (three hard-cover books) may be ordered from the Foundation for Inner Peace, P.O. Box 635, Tiburon, California 94920. Price is $40. All three books are also available in a single soft-cover volume for $25. California residents add 6% sales tax. A cassette tape of readings from Accept This Gift *is available for $9.95 plus tax from Audio Renaissance Tapes, 9110 Sunset Blvd., Suite 200, Los Angeles, California 90069.*

THE DESIRE FOR HEALING

T228. *The Decision to Heal:* T 182; T 215; T 489; T 598, T 214; MT 19; T 350; WB 316. *The Conditions of Healing:* T 553; T 201; T 201; T 160; T 111; T 529; T 535; T 134; T 180; T 535; T 535; T 535; WB 255. *Healing One Another:* T 134; WB 254; WB 261; T 490; WB 255; T 529; T 529; T 530; T 430; WB 364; T 155; T 529; T 366; T 378; T 245; WB 475; T 399.

THE DREAM OF SICKNESS

WB 73. *The Veil of Illusion:* T 188; T 318; T 408; T 591; T 588; MT 23; T 323; T 559. *Separation Is Sickness:* T 207; T 241; WB 421; T 202; MT 54; T 148; MT 17; MT 16; T 182; T 172; T 172; WB 265. *Limitations of the Body:* T 97; T 560; T 140; T 560; T 177; WB 372; T 97; T 140; T 140; T 142; T 143; T 143; T 141; T 146; T 142; T 97; T 301; WB 378. *The World You See:* T 251; T 19; T 539; T 537; T 536; T 212; T 539; T 591; T 536; WB 256; WB 420. *Time and Eternity:* T 240; T 156; T 230; WB 11; T 513; WB 13; T 240; T 324; T 241; T 79; T 178; T 272; T 322; T 282; T 283; T 520; T 235; WB 443; T 519; WB 360; WB 361; WB 360. *From Fear to Faith:* T 110; T 202; P 9; T 152; T 198; T 267; T 172; T 112; T 152; T 112; T 394; T 373; T 374; T 373; WB 435.

THE CAUSES OF THE DREAM

T 543. *Attack and Blame:* T 200; P 19; WB 475; T 272; T 187; T 187; T 187. *Escape from Guilt:* P 10; T 255; T 256; T 217; T 245; T 245; T 263; T 385; T 264; T 263; T 283; T 258. *The Power of Perception:* T 430; T 428; T 214; T 341; WB 329; T 332; T 429; T 123; T 106; T 148; WB 365; WB 454; WB 428; WB 348; WB 429. *Learning and Teaching:* T 275; T 278; T 620; T 183; T 251; T 183; WB 357; WB 325; T 103; T 75; MT 54; MT 45; T 87. *A Change of Mind:* WB 236; P 8; MT 17; T 174; T 148; T 148; T 549; T 175; T 113; T 127; WB 456.

THE MEANS OF AWAKENING

T 147. *Awakening from the Dream:* T 551; T 327; T 551; T 551; WB 263; WB 263; T 551; T 553; T 553; WB 254; WB 263; WB 263; T 213; T 147; WB 255; MT 31. *Looking Within:* T 134; T 573; T 573; P 16; T 249; T 537; T 453; T 15; T 100; T 186; WB 80; WB 416; T 363. *Psychotherapy:* P 1; P 1; P 9; P 3; P 1; T 161; P 13; P 18. *Forgiveness and Gratitude:* MT 53; T 370; WB 175; T 516; T 592; T 593; T 594; WB 370; WB 223; WB 131; WB 131; T 298; T 590; T 76; WB 293; WB 460; T 595; T 396; T 404; WB 363; WB 363; WB 363; WB 363; WB 99; WB 145. *Reality and Truth:* T 159; T 174; T 158; T 199; T 597; WB 264; T 325; WB 255; WB 264; T 196; T 345; WB 189; WB 189; WB 252; WB 254; T 200; WB 469; WB 252; WB 469; WB 253; WB 252.

THE JOY OF FREEDOM

T 198. *The Holy Instant:* T 288; T 325; T 434; T 282; T 358; T 358; T 323. *Vision and Wholeness:* T 218; T 415; WB 91; T 411; T 432; T 621; WB 191; T 413; T 413; T 414; T 413; T 398; T 398; T 398; T 413; WB 292; T 417; T 448; WB 88; T 183; T 235; T 82; T 66; T 147; T 110; T 318; T 187; T 88; T 417; T 417; T 209; T 219; T 246; MT 53; T 243; T 123; T 123. *Love and Joy:* T 198; WB 176; T 203; T 202; T 115; T 227; T 215; T 537; WB 415; T 115; T 198; T 66; T 117; T 66; WB 352; T 66; T 143; WB 183; WB 182; T 180; T 66; T 105; WB 352. *The Light in You:* T 235; T 131; WB 348; T 246; T 247; T 236; T 186; T 233; T 232; T 248; T 235; T 254; T 399; T 256; T 236; T 417; T 450. *Rest in God:* T 109; T 110; P 11; T 502; WB 341; T 240; WB 193; WB 193; WB 193.

PENGUIN

ARKANA

NEW AGE BOOKS FOR MIND, BODY & SPIRIT

With over 200 titles currently in print, Arkana is the leading name in quality books for mind, body and spirit. Arkana encompasses the spirituality of both East and West, ancient and new. A vast range of interests is covered, including Psychology and Transformation, Health, Science and Mysticism, Women's Spirituality, Zen, Western Traditions and Astrology.

If you would like a catalogue of Arkana books, please write to:

Sales Dept. – Arkana
Penguin Books USA Inc.
375 Hudson Street
New York, NY 10014

Arkana Marketing Department
Penguin Books Ltd
27 Wrights Lane
London W8 5TZ